Who Is
Sonia Sotomayor?

by Megan Stine

illustrated by Dede Putra

Grosset & Dunlap
An Imprint of Penguin Random House

For Maddy—MS

Dedicated to my parents—DP

GROSSET & DUNLAP
Penguin Young Readers Group
An Imprint of Penguin Random House LLC

Text copyright © 2017 by Megan Stine. Illustrations copyright © 2017 by Penguin Random House LLC. All rights reserved. Published by Grosset & Dunlap, an imprint of Penguin Random House LLC, 345 Hudson Street, New York, New York 10014. The WHO HQ™ colophon and GROSSET & DUNLAP are trademarks of Penguin Random House LLC. Printed in the USA.

Library of Congress Cataloging-in-Publication Data is available.

ISBN 9780399541926 (paperback)   10 9 8 7 6 5 4 3 2 1
ISBN 9780451533654 (library binding)   10 9 8 7 6 5 4 3 2 1

Contents

Who Is Sonia Sotomayor?

New York City: May 25, 2009

It was a warm spring day—the kind of day to be outside. But Sonia Sotomayor was in her office, sitting beside her phone. She was waiting for the most important call of her life. A call from the White House! She would learn whether President Barack Obama wanted her to be a judge on the Supreme Court.

Sonia was already a judge. Her courtroom was in downtown New York City. But being one of the nine judges on the Supreme Court would be very different.

The Supreme Court is the most important court in the country—it decides whether laws in the United States are fair or not. Its decisions are final.

All day the phone in her office rang again and again. Each time Sonia picked it up, it was her family calling. They wanted to know what was happening. If she got the job, she would be only the third woman to sit on the Supreme Court— and the very first Hispanic person. Her family would be invited to go to the White House with her the next day. Some family members were coming from Puerto Rico!

Finally, at seven o'clock that evening, Sonia couldn't stand waiting any longer. She picked up the phone and called the White House herself.

She spoke to an aide to the president. What should she do? If she was picked, she had to get to Washington by the next morning.

The aide told Sonia to go home and pack—and wait for a call.

Then, a little after 8:00 p.m., the call came, the one she so hoped for. It was the president. He told her he would name her to be the next associate justice on the Supreme Court!

Sonia choked up and started to cry. "Thank you, Mr. President," she said.

Then he asked her to promise two things. He wanted her to stay the same person that she was—and to always stay connected to the world she had come from.

For Sonia Sotomayor—a girl who had grown up poor and proud of her Puerto Rican heritage—that was a promise she was very happy to make.

Latino and Hispanic

What is the difference between the terms *Latino* and *Hispanic*? A boy or man whose family comes from Latin America is called *Latino*. A girl or woman whose family comes from Latin America is *Latina*. *Hispanic* refers to someone whose family comes from a Spanish-speaking place, like Spain, Mexico, or Puerto Rico. So a person like Sonia Sotomayor, whose family comes from Puerto Rico, could be called Hispanic *and* Latina.

LATIN
AMERICA

CHAPTER 1
Born in the Bronx

The five boroughs of New York City

Sonia Maria Sotomayor was born on June 25, 1954. Her parents, Juan and Celina, brought her home. They lived in a poor area of the Bronx, which is part of New York City. Like many of their neighbors, Juan and Celina had come to the

United States from Puerto Rico. They had each left Puerto Rico in 1944, hoping for a better life. In the Bronx, they met and married. They moved into the building where Juan's mother lived.

The Sotomayors worked hard to make a life in their new country. Celina worked at a hospital while she studied to become a nurse. Juan worked in a factory. Celina learned some English, but the family spoke only Spanish at home.

When Sonia was three years old, her brother, Juan, was born. The family called him Junior. With the family growing, her parents decided to move to a bigger, nicer apartment in the Bronx.

Sonia liked her new home but missed living near her grandmother Mercedes. Years later, Sonia wrote a book about her life. She called it *My Beloved World*, and it was published in 2013. In the book, she wrote about her grandmother— how full of life she was. She gave parties for the family almost every Saturday night. Everyone danced, played dominoes, and sang. Mercedes read poetry about Puerto Rico and cooked large meals. The apartment would fill with the smell

of Puerto Rican food like chicken cooked with onions and garlic. Even as a child, Sonia liked pig's feet and pig's ears!

When Sonia was very young, Mercedes began taking her to Puerto Rico for vacations.

Sonia loved those trips. She never forgot the clear blue water of the ocean and the white sandy beaches of Puerto Rico.

Puerto Rico

Puerto Rico is an island in the Atlantic Ocean. It is about one thousand miles from Florida. The name Puerto Rico means "rich port" in Spanish. The island was owned by Spain for 405 years. That is why Spanish is the main language. But ever since 1898, Puerto Rico has been part of the United States.

FLORIDA

PUERTO RICO

Although Puerto Rico is not a state, everyone born in Puerto Rico is an American citizen. But Puerto Ricans do not have all the rights of US citizens. They can't vote for Congress members or for presidents.

Some Puerto Ricans wish their country could become the fifty-first state. Others want Puerto Rico to be an independent nation—not part of the United States. Sonia Sotomayor has thought a lot about this question over the years, but it is tricky to decide.

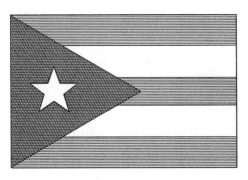

Flag of Puerto Rico

Sonia's father was a sweet man. He took Sonia on picnics, to the beach, and to Yankees games. But he drank too much. Her parents fought a lot because of this.

When Sonia's father lost his job, Celina worked nights and weekends to support the family. She also worked to pay for Sonia and Junior to go to a Catholic school. Celina thought education was the most important thing in the world.

But Sonia didn't like her school. It was called Blessed Sacrament. The nuns were very strict. They slapped kids who didn't behave.

Sonia had other troubles as well. When she was almost eight years old, she fainted in church. And this was not the first sign of a problem. Sonia often had no energy. She was thirsty all the time. She was losing weight. Celina took Sonia to the doctor right away.

The doctor sent Sonia to Prospect Hospital in the Bronx for some tests. Celina worked at Prospect Hospital, so Sonia wasn't afraid at first.

But when the tests were done, the doctor had bad news. Sonia had type I diabetes. Sonia had never seen her mother cry until that moment.

Diabetes Then and Now

People with diabetes have too much sugar in their blood. Their bodies can't get rid of the sugar. There is medicine that keeps the sugar at a safe level. It is called insulin. Insulin is given through injections. The problem is that sugar levels can change very quickly. So people with diabetes have to test their blood all day long. They have to carry insulin with them all the time to give themselves shots. In the early 1960s, when Sonia was young, it was much harder to control diabetes. Many diabetics did not live as long as people without the disease. Today, however, treatment has improved. People like Sonia live much longer and lead active lives.

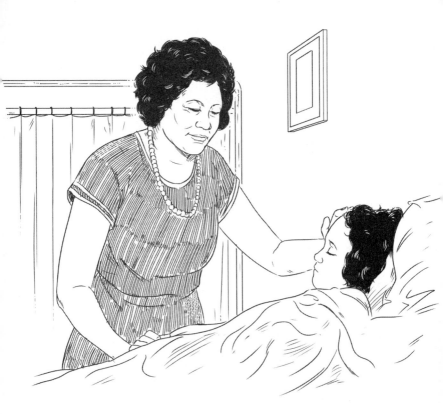

Sonia was scared. She had to stay in the hospital for a week. When she got home from the hospital, Sonia felt better. But there was another problem. As Sonia explained in her book, her parents were nervous about giving her insulin shots. Celina was a nurse, but she hated the idea of hurting Sonia. Her parents started fighting about it.

Sonia was always a girl who wanted to solve problems herself. So she climbed up on a chair near the stove to boil water for sterilizing the needle. (Sterilizing means getting rid of germs.)

At first her mother was worried. Should she really let a young girl use the stove and handle a needle? Nearly all parents would say absolutely not. But Celina decided to trust her child. From that day on, Sonia gave herself shots of insulin every day.

Now that her disease was under control, she had more energy.

But the very next year, her world changed again. Her father died suddenly of a heart attack. He was only forty-two years old.

Sonia and Junior were very sad, but their mother seemed overcome by grief. Years later, Sonia wrote that her mother wouldn't come out of her room at night. How was a nine-year-old girl supposed to have a happy childhood with so much misery around her?

CHAPTER 2
High-School Hopes and Dreams

Sonia was lonely all that summer. With nothing much to do, she turned to books. She spent hours reading in the library. Her favorite books were Nancy Drew mysteries. Sonia loved how Nancy Drew could solve crimes and catch bad guys.

Sonia knew that she might not live very long. Still, she thought a lot about the future. She was determined to make the most of the time she had. She wanted an important career. Maybe she could solve crimes like Nancy Drew . . . or Perry Mason.

Perry Mason was a hit TV show when Sonia was young. It was about a clever lawyer who defended innocent people accused of murder. Every week, Perry Mason would win a case in court.

If she wanted to be a lawyer one day, Sonia knew she'd have to study hard and get good grades.

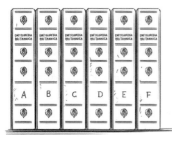

Her mother had taught Sonia the importance of learning. Even though they were poor, Celina bought a set of encyclopedias for their home. The thick, leather-bound books were the kind that most people only saw in libraries. Sonia paged through a different volume each day, learning as much as she could.

School became easier after Sonia's father died. The nuns were kinder to Sonia now. And Celina started speaking English at home. That helped a lot.

Sonia also learned that asking for help was a great way to succeed. One day she asked one of the smartest girls in school for help. The girl gave Sonia some study tips. After that, Sonia got better grades.

By the time Sonia was ready to start high school, her Bronx neighborhood had become a rough place. It was full of drug dealers and gangs. So Celina moved the family to a safer part of the Bronx. Their new apartment was near Cardinal Spellman High School. That's where Sonia started ninth grade.

When Sonia was first at Cardinal Spellman, the girls and boys did not have classes together. They only saw one another at lunch. Still, Sonia made plenty of friends. She also had a boyfriend named Kevin Noonan.

Kevin had blue-gray eyes and curly light brown hair. He was smart and interesting. He made Sonia feel special.

Kevin Noonan

On their first date, Kevin took Sonia to a fancy part of Manhattan. It was only a subway ride away from the Bronx. But as Sonia wrote later, it seemed like a whole different world.

After that first date, Sonia and Kevin became a couple. He spent as much time as he could at Sonia's house.

Ken Moy

Sonia had other good friends at school, too. Ken Moy was a year older than Sonia. She met him when she joined a club where students had to make speeches. Ken coached her on how to speak in front of an audience. Sonia knew that would help her become a lawyer—just like Perry Mason.

All through high school, Sonia studied hard. She also worked at Prospect Hospital. Junior worked as well—he had two jobs! They both had to help out because the family was so poor.

Junior Sotomayor

27

With so little money, Sonia wasn't sure how she would ever pay for college. Then one day, when Sonia was a senior, her friend Ken Moy called. Ken was now at Princeton University. Princeton was in the Ivy League, a small group of top schools in the country.

Ken gave Sonia some advice.

"Try for the Ivy League," he said. It might be hard for Sonia to fit in, especially being poor and Hispanic. But he said an Ivy League education would change her life forever.

Sonia decided to take Ken's advice. She applied to three Ivy League schools—Harvard, Yale, and Princeton. She had no idea how tough it was to get into these schools. But guess what? She was accepted at all three!

After visiting each, Sonia decided to follow in Ken Moy's footsteps. She would go to Princeton. The college was in New Jersey, only about an hour and a half from New York City.

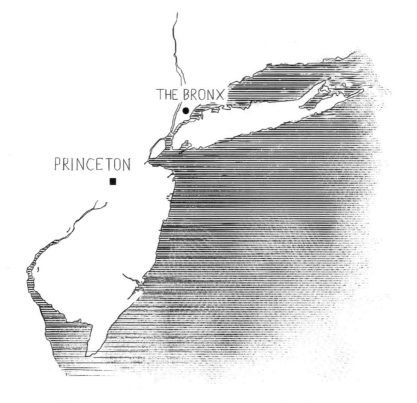

But for Sonia, Princeton was completely new and different—like nowhere she'd ever been before.

CHAPTER 3
Princeton

At Princeton, many of the students came from rich families. Most were white. By college many had traveled all over the world. They went skiing, owned fancy cars, and wore expensive clothes.

They felt right at home on the beautiful college campus, with its fancy wood-paneled dining halls and old stone buildings.

But Princeton wanted more students from different backgrounds. They were trying to bring in smart, hardworking students like Sonia Sotomayor. It was part of a program called Affirmative Action.

Affirmative Action

Affirmative Action is a program that helps minorities get ahead in school and find work. It started in the United States in the 1960s. It was a way to make up for racial discrimination. If two people applied for a job, most of the time the white person would be chosen over the black one. Affirmative Action tried to change that. In 1961, President John F. Kennedy signed a law that required anyone working for the government to take positive action—affirmative action—to make sure minorities could get government jobs. When minorities applied for a job—or applied for college—they were given extra consideration because they were in a minority. That way, people who had not been as lucky growing up were given a better chance to succeed.

Princeton gave Sonia a full scholarship. That meant she didn't have to pay for school. Without the scholarship, she could never have afforded to be at Princeton. Sonia has said many times over the years that she was grateful for Affirmative Action. It helped her get into a top school and achieve her dreams.

Soon enough, Sonia had a group of friends. Her roommate, Dolores, was Mexican American. They hung out together on campus at the Third World Center. It was a center for minority students.

Most of the people Sonia met there were interested in politics and justice. They wanted to make the world a better place. Years later, First Lady Michelle Obama would go to Princeton. She spent much of her time at the Third World Center, too.

Sonia didn't get good grades at first. To her surprise, she got a C on the first paper she wrote for a history class. So she did what she had done before—she asked for help. Her professor explained how to write more clearly and put forth a convincing argument on paper.

Other professors helped, too. They told her that she was mixing Spanish grammar into English sentences. So in the summer after her freshman year, Sonia bought some English grammar books. She studied them hard. After that, her grades improved.

Meanwhile, Sonia and Kevin were still a couple. Kevin had gone off to a different college. He came to visit Sonia on weekends.

Even though she was getting good grades now, Sonia didn't always feel like she fit in. It was hard being one of only a handful of Hispanics on campus.

Feeling like an outsider made Sonia determined to change things at Princeton. One thing Sonia noticed was that Princeton had no Hispanic professors. Not one. Even the Spanish classes weren't taught by Hispanic people.

She and her friends from the Third World Center wrote letters to the people in charge of

Princeton. Then she wrote to the US government. She sent in a complaint. Her complaint was that Princeton was being unfair to minorities.

It worked! After that, Princeton hired a Hispanic person for an important job—as assistant dean of student affairs.

By the time Sonia was ready to graduate, she was known as a leader, someone who took charge. And her grades were excellent. Yet as graduation grew closer, Sonia realized she still had a lot to learn.

One day, Sonia walked into her dorm room. As she explained years later in the book about her life, Sonia found her friend Felice sitting there.

Felice looked embarrassed. She had seen a letter in Sonia's wastebasket. It was an invitation to join a very special club called Phi Beta Kappa. The club was only for the very top students. At Princeton, that meant the best of the best! Sonia had thrown the letter away because she had never heard of Phi Beta Kappa.

Sonia took Felice's advice. She answered the invitation and got a Phi Beta Kappa key—a symbol of the club's honor.

In June of 1976, Sonia graduated from Princeton. Besides Phi Beta Kappa, she received other honors, as well. She was the cowinner of the Pyne Prize—the highest award a senior at Princeton could receive.

Finishing college was really just the start of her education, however. Sonia realized she would keep on learning for the rest of her life.

CHAPTER 4
Law and Marriage

Everyone in the Sotomayor family expected Sonia and Kevin to get married. Sonia and Kevin expected it, too. They had been sweethearts since high school, after all.

So in the summer after college graduation, they planned their wedding. This was the right time. In the fall, Sonia would be starting law school at Yale. Her childhood dream of becoming a lawyer was going to come true!

Yale Law School

St. Patrick's Cathedral

The wedding was held on August 14, 1976, at St. Patrick's Cathedral in New York City. St. Patrick's is a huge, beautiful church on Fifth Avenue. How did Sonia and Kevin get married in such a fancy place? Junior, her brother, worked for the church!

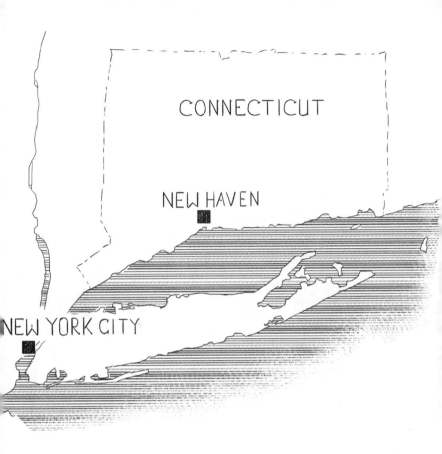

After the wedding, Sonia and Kevin moved to New Haven, Connecticut. That's where Yale Law School is. For the next three years, Sonia studied law. Kevin got a job in a science lab. Sonia worked part-time jobs, too. One of her jobs was as a bouncer in a campus bar!

Sonia had to make sure everyone was old enough and no one came in without paying. She was strict about the rules.

Law school was hard—harder than Sonia had expected. She had to study all the time. Once again she felt she had to prove herself. Just like at Princeton, there weren't many Latino students or other minorities. Affirmative Action had helped Sonia get into Yale Law School.

At Yale Law School, Latino people held some important jobs. In her first year there, Sonia met Jose Cabranes. He was a legend to many Puerto Ricans. Once he had been a lawyer for the governor of Puerto Rico. Now he worked at Yale as their top lawyer.

Jose Cabranes

Quickly, Cabranes became a mentor to Sonia—a person who gave her advice and helped her career. Sonia worked part-time for Cabranes. She also learned a lot just by watching him. Sonia saw how he spoke and acted in front of people. He was smart, kind, and generous. He also cared deeply about the things he believed in—like the future of Puerto Rico. Cabranes was a Hispanic person from a poor background who was treated with a huge amount of respect.

For Sonia, law school was a lot like Princeton. She started out slowly, not sure of herself. At first, she never raised her hand in class. But by her final year of law school, she was doing well. She wrote an article for the *Yale Law Journal*—and it was printed! Only the best students had articles in the *Journal*.

In October 1978, Sonia and other students were invited to have dinner with lawyers from a big law firm in Washington, DC. The law firm was looking to hire Yale grads. Sonia understood that the dinner was like a job interview. If the lawyers were impressed with her, she might be offered a job.

But the dinner didn't go well. The man sitting across from Sonia was one of the heads of the law firm. The very first words out of his mouth were about Affirmative Action. Did Sonia get into Yale because she was Puerto Rican?

Yes, Sonia said. She was grateful that Yale Law School wanted more students of color. Being Latina had helped her get accepted.

The man thought it was a big problem. He said law firms shouldn't hire Affirmative Action students. Why? Because they'd just end up firing them a few years later!

Sonia was shocked. The man assumed she wasn't as good as the other Yale students. He'd actually said so to her face!

Sonia never took things lying down. She was a fighter. She made a formal complaint to Yale. She said Yale shouldn't allow that law firm to interview law students on campus—not if they were going to treat Hispanics unfairly. Eventually, the law firm apologized—but they didn't offer Sonia a job. She didn't want to work for them anyway.

Now what? Sonia wondered. She would be graduating from law school soon. But she had no job offers.

Then one night in the law library, she spotted a room full of people. Cheese and crackers were being served. Sonia was hungry, so she went in.

She also wanted to find out what was going on. That's when she met the person who could offer her the perfect job—the job she had been dreaming about since childhood.

CHAPTER 5
Catching the Bad Guys

The man Sonia met in the law library that night was Robert Morgenthau. He was the district attorney, or DA, for New York County. DAs are lawyers who work for a city or county. They bring charges against criminals, put them on trial, and try to send them to jail. DAs are also called prosecutors.

Robert Morgenthau

Morgenthau was famous in New York. He was a tough prosecutor. The night Sonia met him, he was visiting Yale. He was trying to hire Yale Law School graduates to come work for him in New York City.

Sonia listened to what he had to say. He explained that in most big law firms, young lawyers had to wait years before they got a chance to go to court. But in his office, new lawyers prosecuted criminals their first year on the job. Sonia loved the idea of going to court and speaking to juries—just like Perry Mason.

Morgenthau liked Sonia right away and soon offered her a job. Working in the DA's office didn't pay very much. Not compared to the money she could make at a big law firm. Still, it paid a lot more than Sonia's mother had ever earned. And it was work that she felt she was cut out to do.

In 1979, Sonia joined the New York City

DA's office. She would be one of three hundred assistant DAs!

New York City was full of crime then. Thousands of people were arrested every day. The assistant DAs had to decide which crimes were important enough to prosecute.

There was a lot to learn about being a DA— and none of it had been taught in law school.

Sonia had to learn on the job. She was given just a few weeks of training. She learned how the court system worked and how to bring charges against criminals. The new assistant DAs also had practice sessions, which were called "mock trials." Sonia learned how to talk to a jury and convince them that she was right.

Her first real case in court involved a young college student who had been in a street fight.

Sonia described this case when she wrote about it in her book. She said when she stood in front of the judge that day, she stammered. She didn't feel ready. The judge was using words she didn't even understand!

Sonia lost her first case. But she didn't let that stop her. She knew what to do—ask for help and learn more. She won her second case. In fact, she did so well that her bosses considered her a star. Usually, the new DAs handled small crimes for a long time before they were given more important cases. But Sonia moved up very fast.

The work was hard in the New York DA's office, and the hours were long. Every week, Sonia had to spend one whole day talking to police officers about their arrests. Once a month she had to stay in court all day and into the night—till 2:00 a.m.! Working such long hours, Sonia had to be careful about her diabetes. She had to make sure she ate properly so she wouldn't faint in court.

Her office was tiny and unpleasant. It was usually too hot or too cold. At first, she didn't even have an office. Her desk was in a doorway. Still, most of the time, Sonia enjoyed the work. She liked winning cases. But she also knew when it was right to drop the charges. Her bosses had taught her how to be tough but fair. They trusted her judgment.

In 1982, Sonia handled one of the biggest cases of her career as a DA. It was called the Tarzan murder case. The criminal was a man named Richard Maddicks. He robbed apartments by swinging on a rope like Tarzan. He burst through the windows! If someone was home when he broke in, he shot them.

Sonia was chosen to help out on the case. She had to interview the witnesses—just like a detective. And just like Nancy Drew, she found a clue that helped prove Maddicks was guilty!

Her smart work helped put the Tarzan murderer in jail.

But even though she liked being a DA, the job was taking a toll on her. She and Kevin hardly spent any time together. They didn't have as much in common now, either. In 1983, Sonia and Kevin divorced. They weren't mad at each other. They had simply grown up, and grown apart.

Now Sonia had to start a new life—on her own.

CHAPTER 6
Moving Up and Moving On

After her divorce, Sonia got an apartment in Brooklyn near friends from work. During the week, she and her friends worked very hard. But on weekends, they had parties and went to concerts and the theater. Sonia rented a house at the beach.

She knew her life might be short because of her diabetes. Sonia wanted to live fully and do as much as she could with the time she had.

One way to live fully, Sonia decided, was to have new and different experiences. She decided to move on to another job.

So in 1984, she took a job at a law firm called Pavia & Harcourt.

Sonia's job there was exciting and glamorous. She was to help an Italian company called Fendi.

 Fendi made expensive handbags that were sold all over the world. But in the 1980s, fake Fendi bags started popping up in New York. Criminals sold these copies on the street for very low prices. Why would someone pay $350 for a purse if, for $45, they could buy one that looked almost the same? Every time someone bought a fake bag, Fendi lost money.

Sonia went to court. She got a judge to agree that the criminals should be stopped. The court gave her permission to "seize" the fake bags. That meant she was legally allowed to go out on the streets and take all the fake bags away from the criminals. It was dangerous work. So Sonia didn't do it alone. A group of former police officers went with her.

The problem was that the criminals were tough. Sometimes they fought back! Sometimes they grabbed their fake stuff and ran away. Sonia and the police had to chase after them.

Over time, the bad guys began to recognize Sonia. They threatened to hurt her. Sonia had to wear a bulletproof vest!

Some of the younger lawyers who worked with Sonia were afraid to go out on raids with her. But Sonia loved the raids. One time, she and the police seized twenty-three thousand handbags!

The Fendi family who owned the business invited her to Rome. They also took Sonia all over Europe. They showed her what life was like for people who were rich and famous. Still, Sonia remained true to her roots.

She invited the Fendis to come to her mother's home for Thanksgiving dinner in the Bronx. She was never ashamed of her humble beginnings. She was proud of her family and her past.

In 1988, the lawyers who owned Pavia & Harcourt took a vote. They decided to make Sonia a partner in the law firm. Now she was one of the bosses. She earned a big salary, had a great job, and traveled all over the world.

What more could she want?

In the back of her mind, Sonia had always wanted one more thing. She didn't tell anyone, but secretly she wanted to be a judge.

CHAPTER 7
Your Honor

Sonia thought she was keeping it secret—her dream of becoming a judge. But somehow, the older, more experienced lawyers in her life seemed to know. They gave her advice that would help her achieve her goal.

Jose Cabranes, her mentor, told her to do volunteer work for Puerto Rican groups that needed lawyers. David Botwinick, one of the nine partners at Pavia & Harcourt, helped Sonia get an important volunteer job with the state of New York. Then her old boss, Robert Morgenthau, stepped in. He asked the mayor of New York to put Sonia on a committee that looked at how money was spent in political campaigns.

All of her volunteer jobs gave Sonia a chance to be noticed by politicians. And guess who appointed judges to the biggest, most important courts? Politicians!

When the time was right, David Botwinick encouraged Sonia to apply to be a US district court judge. The US district court was not like the state courts where criminals were put on trial. It was not like the court where Sonia had been a prosecutor. It was a higher court, in charge of the most important kinds of cases. The judges—not juries—made the decisions.

Wow! Sonia thought. Being a judge on the district court? That would be incredible. But Sonia was only thirty-six years old! What were the chances she would be chosen?

It took Sonia nearly a week to fill out the application. She had to explain everything about her life—every person she knew, every case she'd worked on, every volunteer job she'd held.

The Court System

The court system in America can be confusing. There are so many different kinds of courts.

- Local courts in towns and cities handle small problems. Traffic courts deal with people who get tickets for driving too fast. Family courts help settle problems when people get divorced.

New York City Family Court

- State courts handle bigger crimes. Juries decide whether the person is guilty or not.

- Federal courts deal with laws that apply to the whole country. If someone makes counterfeit money, that's a federal crime. It is illegal in every state.

  There are three "layers" in the federal court system.

- The "lowest" federal court is the US district court. There are ninety-four district courts across the country. The district court in New York is one of the most important because so many big cases start in New York City.

- The next highest federal court is called the circuit court. This is where lawyers go to appeal rulings (that means they try to change the verdict) of the lower court. Cases are decided by a group of judges, usually three.

- The highest court in the land is the Supreme Court. It is the last chance to reverse a lower court's ruling. There are nine justices (another name for judges) on the Supreme Court.

They are appointed for life. When one of them dies or retires, the president suggests to Congress who should fill the job. But Congress has to approve the president's recommendation.

Senator Patrick Moynihan

Sonia sent the job application to Senator Patrick Moynihan. He was the New York senator who would recommend her.

But that was only the beginning. She would have to be interviewed by a lot of people. She would have to answer questions in front of Congress. Then Congress would have to vote. If they didn't approve her, Sonia wouldn't become a judge.

Do you think all these steps happened quickly? No. The process took almost two years!

Finally, in 1992, Congress approved her. President George H. W. Bush named her as a federal judge. Her court would be the US District Court for the Southern District of New York, which covered eight counties in lower New York.

New York State Supreme Court Building

THE TRUE ADMINISTRATION OF JUSTICE IS THE FIRMEST PILLAR OF GOOD GOVERNMENT

It was an incredible honor and a dream come true. Best of all, she could stay in this job forever. Federal judges were appointed for life.

Learning to be a judge was just like everything else Sonia had done. She had to dive in and learn fast, on the job.

Years later, Sonia admitted that at first she was scared to sit in the courtroom. She tried to handle all her cases in her office, which is called the judge's chambers. But finally she had to go into court and sit on the bench. She put on her judge's black robe. She was so nervous, her knees knocked together!

JUDGE SONIA SOTOMAYOR

Pretty soon, though, Sonia felt confident being a judge.

In 1995, she had to decide one of the biggest cases of the year.

The case was about baseball.

All Major League Baseball players had gone out on strike. They didn't like the deal that the team owners were offering them. The strike had been going on for seven months. There had been no World Series the year before!

Sonia was the judge for the case. The day of the trial, TV cameras and reporters filled the halls outside the courtroom. Sonia listened to the lawyers for each side. Then she took a short break.

Some people thought Judge Sotomayor would take days or weeks to decide the case. But Sonia loved baseball just as much as everyone else. She was a big fan of the New York Yankees. She didn't want the strike to drag on. Spring training was just around the corner.

So she gave her decision right away. She was kind and polite to everyone. But she agreed with the players. The owners were being unfair. She said the owners should keep working with the players for a new contract. When the players heard her ruling, they ended the strike. Sonia Sotomayor had saved baseball!

The *New York Times* wrote about Sonia. They said she was like a great baseball player who could "wake up on Christmas Day and pull a curve ball."

That meant she didn't need any spring training—or practice—to do her job well.

Sonia probably didn't agree with that, though. Hard work and practice had always been the keys to her success—in everything she did.

CHAPTER 8
Higher and Higher

Life was good for Judge Sotomayor. She loved her work and her friends. The people who worked for her were like a second family. Sometimes she invited them home with her to have burgers and play cards.

Her diabetes was under control now, too. She was very careful about what she ate. She always took her insulin when she needed it. She sometimes gave herself shots at meals, right in front of people.

Sonia's life could have gone on like that forever.

But on June 25, 1997, she got a call from President Bill Clinton. He wanted to appoint her to a higher court— the US Court of Appeals for the Second Circuit.

Bill Clinton

Sonia knew what that meant. It meant she would have to go through a lot of interviews— again. She would have to answer questions in front of Congress—again. Then Congress would have to vote to approve her. The whole thing could take a long time. But it was a huge honor. It was also a signal that someday a president might choose her for the Supreme Court!

As before, Senator Moynihan stood up for Sonia in Congress. So did the other senator from New York, Alfonse D'Amato. Ten thousand people wrote letters to support her.

Still, Congress stalled. For a long time, they wouldn't vote. Why not? Was it because some congressmen didn't want a Hispanic woman to have a chance at being on the Supreme Court someday?

Senator Al D'Amato

The stalling trick was used a lot—especially when appointing people of color. Other nominees became judges quite quickly, but minorities and women often had to wait two or three years.

Finally, though, in October 1998, the Senate voted in favor of Sonia.

On November 6, there was a swearing-in ceremony. Many famous people were there. So were Sonia's family and friends.

The twelve other judges from the Second Circuit Court were there, too—including Jose Cabranes. He was now an important judge himself, and he swore her in. In court, she would be sitting right alongside him.

After the ceremony, Sonia and her family celebrated. And that night, there was another special event. Sonia's mother, Celina, was getting married. She was in love with a man named Omar Lopez. Sonia, as a judge, performed their marriage ceremony.

Sonia had a wonderful job, close family, and dear friends. There was nothing more she could ask for or expect.

Or was there?

CHAPTER 9
One of Nine

For the next ten years, Sonia not only served as a judge, she also taught classes at six different law schools. She gave speeches all over the country.

Then, one day in 2009, she got a call from the White House. One of the nine Supreme Court justices was going to retire. President Barack Obama would have to pick a replacement.

"Do not tell anyone," the White House told Sonia.

Sonia was on the "short list" of people President Obama was considering. There were three other people on the list. Sonia knew what this meant. If she was nominated, there would be more interviews. More questions from Congress. More waiting. Finally, the Senate would have to vote.

The Supreme Court

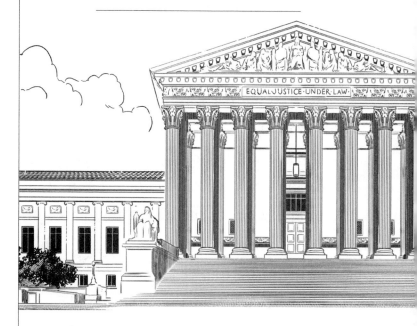

The Supreme Court is one of three branches of the US government. It is the judiciary branch. The other two branches are the executive (the president) and the legislative (Congress).

Each branch has different powers. The Supreme Court has the power to decide whether laws are fair, according to our Constitution.

There are nine justices on the Supreme Court—an uneven number. That way, there can never be a tie vote. (There are no juries to decide cases at the Supreme Court.) The justices all listen to each case.

Then they vote on how to rule. Sometimes the justices agree, but they often disagree. Some votes are five to four. That means only five people agreed about how to rule on the case. The other four disagreed. The majority always wins. Supreme Court judges are appointed for life.

But it would be even harder this time. Senators are very careful about voting for Supreme Court justices. Why? Because the Supreme Court has a lot of power. It makes decisions about big issues that affect everyone, every day. As for Sonia, she worried about how being on the Supreme Court could change her life. She would be famous. She wouldn't have much privacy. Was it worth it?

The Supreme Court in 2008

Yes, Sonia decided. She wanted to try. She wanted minority children to know that they were just like her. They could grow up to achieve their biggest dreams if they worked hard enough.

The next few months were crazy. First, FBI agents came to visit. They asked questions about her life. The president wanted to be sure Sonia didn't have any problems or ugly secrets in her past. The White House also called her doctor to ask

about her diabetes. The president needed to know that Sonia would be healthy enough to serve on the Supreme Court for many years.

Next, Sonia went to the White House to meet the president in person. That day she also met Vice President Joe Biden and many members of the White House staff.

Finally she was told to wait for a phone call on May 25.

When it came a little after 8:00 p.m., Sonia

was thrilled. But she had to hurry! Somehow, she had to get from New York City to Washington, DC, that night. The White House didn't want her to fly. They were afraid reporters would find out. They wanted to keep it a big secret until the next day.

So a friend of Sonia's drove her to Washington, DC, in a rainstorm. They didn't arrive till after 2:00 a.m. Her mother, brother, and other family members were already there. Some family members had even flown in from Puerto Rico to be part of this historic event.

The next morning, Sonia and her family stood in the East Room of the White House with President Obama. Reporters and TV cameras were there. President Obama announced that he was naming her as the next Supreme Court justice. She would be only the third woman, and first Hispanic, ever to sit on the court.

Then Sonia made a short speech. She said that as a child, she had never imagined—even in her wildest dreams—this would happen.

For the next few weeks, Sonia's life was a whirlwind. She had to get ready for the Senate hearings. Those were the meetings when senators would ask her questions. The hearings would be on television. If she didn't answer questions well, she would look bad. The senators might not vote for her.

Sonia decided to try to meet as many senators as she could ahead of time. Of the hundred US senators, she met with eighty-nine!

On one visit to Washington, DC, she tripped in the airport and fractured her ankle. That didn't stop her. She limped into the White House. Later that day, she had a cast put on her leg. One senator even signed her cast.

The hearings were scheduled for July 2009. The White House helped Sonia get ready. They held practice sessions—sometimes for ten hours a day!

They told her what suits to wear each day, and what color nail polish to use. Sonia liked bright red nails. The White House told her to use a plain color instead.

On the first day of the hearings, Sonia sat alone at a big table. In front of her were sixteen senators. They sat up high behind a raised desk. It looked like a courtroom. The senators questioned her over and over, for four long days.

Finally the hearings were over.

Three weeks later, on August 6, 2009, the Senate voted. They agreed to put Sonia Sotomayor on the Supreme Court.

On August 8, she was sworn in to the Supreme Court—twice! One ceremony was private. The other was in front of photographers and reporters. Chief Justice John Roberts gave her the oath both times. Sonia put her hand on a Bible while Celina held it, smiling.

After that, the celebrating and the parties began. Many famous people wanted to congratulate Sonia. Two people wrote songs for Sonia. President Obama had a party for her at the White House. Jennifer Lopez, the famous singer, also had a big party at her mansion on Long Island, New York. J-Lo and Sonia were both from Puerto Rican families. They had both grown up in the Bronx.

Although Sonia had already been sworn in as a judge, there was one more ceremony to be held. It wouldn't be official until then.

The night before the ceremony, Sonia went out partying and dancing with her family. Even though she was about to become a Supreme Court justice, she didn't want to start acting differently. She danced the salsa and sang in front of the whole crowd. After all, that's what President Obama had asked her to do—stay herself. Stay connected to the world she had come from.

The ceremony was held the next day, September 8. It took only four minutes. Sonia sat in her robes on the bench in the Supreme Court for the first time. She felt humble and proud—and in awe of the world she was about to enter.

Omar, Celina, Sonia, sister-in-law Tracey, and Junior

The Supreme Court opened the day after Sonia was sworn in. (The court is in session from the first Monday in October to late June or early July.) Ruth Bader Ginsburg had a habit of wearing a lace collar with her black judge's robe. She gave Sonia Sotomayor a similar lace collar to wear on her first day on the court. Sonia wore it for a while, but then stopped. She isn't really the lacy type.

Women of the Supreme Court

The first woman appointed to the Supreme Court was Sandra Day O'Connor. President Ronald Reagan appointed her in 1981. She retired in 2006.

Ruth Bader Ginsburg was the second woman on the court. She was appointed in 1993 by President Bill Clinton.

In 2010, President Obama appointed the fourth woman to the Supreme Court—Justice Elena Kagan.

Sonia took her place among the other eight justices. Her knees were shaking. As always, she wasn't sure she was ready for the job. But as always, she knew what to do—jump in, learn fast, and work hard. That's what she had always done—at Catholic school, at Princeton, and at Yale. It's what she had done in the DA's office in New York, and at her law firm. She had done it when learning to sit on a judge's bench.

It's what her mother had taught her to do, by example. Sonia had been doing it her whole life.

Why stop now?

Some Major Supreme Court Cases

The Supreme Court has decided some very important cases over the years. In 1954, the court decided that it was not legal to make black children attend different schools from white children. The case was called Brown v. Board of Education.

Another important case was called Miranda v. Arizona. In that case, the Supreme Court said that criminal suspects had certain rights when they were arrested, including the right to remain silent and to have a lawyer.

Recently, the Supreme Court settled a big case about gay marriage, Obergfell v. Hodges. The court said that same-sex couples have a right to get married in all fifty states. The vote was five to four in favor. Sonia Sotomayor voted for it, along with four other justices.

Timeline of Sonia Sotomayor's Life

1954	Born in New York City on June 25
1957	Brother Juan is born, family moves to Bronxdale Houses housing project
1961	Diagnosed with diabetes
1963	Father dies
1972	Graduates from Cardinal Spellman High School
1976	Graduates from Princeton University
	Marries Kevin Noonan
1979	Earns law degree from Yale Law School
	Hired as assistant district attorney in New York City
1983	Gets divorced
1984	Joins Pavia & Harcourt law firm
1992	Appointed a US district court judge
1995	Ends Major League Baseball strike
1997	Becomes a judge on the United States Court of Appeals for the Second Circuit
2009	Sworn in as a justice on the Supreme Court
2013	*My Beloved World* is published

Timeline of the World

1898 —	United States takes military control of Puerto Rico
1921 —	Discovery of insulin
1952 —	Puerto Rico becomes a US commonwealth
1961 —	The Berlin Wall built
1966 —	National Organization for Women (NOW) founded
1971 —	Computer floppy disks introduced
1974 —	US president Richard Nixon resigns
1981 —	The first woman, Sandra Day O'Connor, is appointed to the US Supreme Court
1987 —	The Simpsons appear on TV for the first time
1994–1995 —	Major League Baseball strike
1997 —	The British return Hong Kong to China
2005 —	YouTube is invented
2008 —	Barack Obama becomes the first African American person ever elected president of the United States
2009 —	The New York Yankees win their twenty-seventh World Series championship
2012 —	Barack Obama reelected president of the United States

Bibliography

* Books for young readers

* Anderson, Annmarie. ***When I Grow Up: Sonia Sotomayor.*** New York: Scholastic, Inc., 2014.

Collins, Lauren. "Number Nine." ***The New Yorker***, January 11, 2010.

Felix, Antonia. ***Sonia Sotomayor: The True American Dream.*** New York: Berkley Books, 2010.

Greene, Meg. ***Sonia Sotomayor: A Biography.*** Santa Barbara, CA: Greenwood Biographies, 2012.

Powell, Michael. "To Get to Sotomayor's Core, Start in New York." ***New York Times***, July 9, 2009.

Sotomayor, Sonia. ***My Beloved World.*** New York: Vintage Books, 2013.

Stolberg, Sheryl Gay. "Sotomayor, a Trailblazer and a Dreamer." ***New York Times***, May 26, 2009.

Totenberg, Nina. "Sotomayor Found Her 'Competitive Spirit' in Gold Stars." ***All Things Considered***, NPR, January 14, 2013.

Winfrey, Oprah. ***Oprah Talks to Sonia Sotomayor.*** New York: Hearst Corporation, 2013.